JIGSAW PUZZLE LEADERSHIP

GERALD M. DEW, DMin

ISBN: 978-1-60414-903-6

Published by
Fideli Publishing Inc.
119 W. Morgan St.
Martinsville, IN 46151

www.FideliPublishing.com

TABLE OF CONTENTS

ACKNOWLEDGEMENTS

I thank God who kept prodding me to put on paper these ideas that have been especially beneficial to me. I am extremely grateful to my wife, Marva, who helped keep me focused throughout the writing process and who served as a source of strength and encouragement.

I also am in debt to Dr. Ralph D. West, Pastor, The Church Without Walls; Dr. James N. Kent, Professor, Northern Seminary; Dr. Frank A. Thomas, Professor of Homelitics, Christian Theological Seminary; and Reverend James Brooks, Pastor, Harmony Community Church, all of whom played a key role at some point in the development and writing of this book.

FOREWORD

Pastor Gerald Dew has created a great resource for church leaders at all levels. At a time when churches are experiencing generational shifts, rapid change, economic challenges, and polarizing influences, Dew has developed an approach for church leaders to identify and develop leadership attributes in their parishioners. He has included solid tools in *Jigsaw Puzzle Leadership*, which can be used by pastors and lay leaders alike to train current and future teachers and leaders in their ministries.

God never intended for pastors to be the only leaders in churches. The apostle Paul encouraged pastors to work hard to "equip the saints" to lead in the work of the church at all levels. *Jigsaw Puzzle Leadership* will guide pastors to train leaders and leaders to train others for the wide variety of ministries within local churches and Christian ministries. It will also help pastors prepare church leaders and church leaders to prepare others to grow into new ministries and responsibilities as they mature in their Christian faith.

While our culture is embroiled in reactivity and polarization, Dew has developed a manual to help train a new generation of leaders in a manner which will literally help put the pieces back together. Our faith in Christ is all about bringing people together, bridging gaps, and overcoming differences. Dew's work presents methods to help church leaders develop unity without creating uniformity.

One of the most important tasks of leadership development is to assist new leaders in undertaking responsibilities which are a good fit for their spiritual gifts, aptitudes, and abilities. Dew has included excellent tools which can be used to help developing leaders assess their personal attributes and preferences. The inventories included in this book are time tested and user friendly. They will not only help learners to assess and apply their gifts, but learn to use their personalities and aptitudes as attributes for leadership.

People who assemble jigsaw puzzles need to be both patient and persistent. Those who shepherd God's people know if sheep stay too long in one place the sheep starve, and if they try to move the sheep too fast they risk losing some of them along the way. Effective leaders bring people together and move them forward, from one place to a better place.

I hope you find *Jigsaw Puzzle Leadership* as encouraging and practical as I have found it to be.

James N. Kent
Affiliate Professor of Ministry and DMin Thesis Director
Northern Seminary
Lombard, Illinois

JIGSAW PUZZLE LEADERSHIP

I have been in pastoral ministry for a little more than 30 years and I must admit that I have had my share of puzzling situations. I have experienced being bewildered, confounded, perplexed, baffled, and mystified by the challenge of doing the work of the Lord in the land of the devil.

I have also seen churches and ministries go through the same puzzling experiences and emotions. Puzzled by the challenges of winning the lost, making disciples, retaining new members, providing relevant ministry, succession planning, funding the ministry, building and maintaining facilities, managing multiple services and/or multiple sites, and the list goes on and on. Then, as if by divine revelation, it dawned on me one day that what I was dealing with was a puzzle, a jigsaw puzzle with irregular shaped pieces (members) that were made to fit together and form something beautiful.

According to the American Jigsaw Puzzle Society the first jigsaw puzzle was created around 1760 by John Spilsbury, a London engraver and mapmaker. Spilsbury mounted one of his maps on a sheet of hardwood and cut around the borders of the countries using a fine-bladed marquetry saw. The end product was an educational pastime, designed as an aid in teaching British children geography. The idea caught on and, until about 1820, jigsaw puzzles remained primarily educational tools.

In 1880, with the introduction of the treadle saw, what had previously been known as dissections (not a word with particularly enjoyable connotations in our own time) came to be known as jigsaw puzzles, although they were actually cut by a fretsaw, not a true jigsaw. Towards the end of the century plywood came to be used. With illustrations glued or painted on the front of the wood, pencil tracings of where to cut were made on the back. These pencil tracings can still be found on some of these older puzzles.

Cardboard puzzles were first introduced in the late 1800s, and were primarily used for children's puzzles. It was not until the 20th century that cardboard puzzles came to be die-cut, a process whereby thin strips of metal with sharpened edges — rather like a giant cookiecutter — are twisted into intricate patterns and fastened to a plate. The "die" (which refers to this assembly of twisted metal on the plate) is placed in a press, which is pressed down on the cardboard to make the cut.

Thus, in the early 1900s both wooden and cardboard jigsaw puzzles were available. Wooden puzzles still dominated, as manufacturers were convinced that customers would not be interested in "cheap" cardboard puzzles. Of course, a second motivation on the part of manufacturers and retailers of jigsaw puzzles was that the profit from a wooden puzzle, which might sell for $1.00, was far greater than for a cardboard jigsaw puzzle, which would usually sell for about 25¢.

The Golden Age of jigsaw puzzles came in the 1920s and 1930s with companies like Chad Valley and Victory in Great Britain and Einson-Freeman, Viking and others in the United States producing a wide range of puzzles reflecting both the desire for sentimental scenes, enthusiasm for the new technologies in rail and shipping and last but not least, new marketing strategies.

One strategy was to make cardboard puzzles more intricate and difficult, thus appealing as much to adults as to children. Another was to use jigsaw puzzles as premiums for advertising purposes. Einson-Freeman of Long Island City, New York began this practice in 1931, making puzzles that were given away with toothbrushes.

Other premiums followed, but more important to the jigsaw puzzle's enduring success was the introduction of the weekly puzzle. This practice began in the United States in September, 1932 — very much the depth of the Depression — with an initial printing of 12,000 puzzles. Soon after, printings rose to 100,000 and then 200,000.

It might seem odd at first glance that a non-necessity like a jigsaw puzzle would sell so well in the Depression. But the appeal, then as now, was that one bought a good deal of entertainment for a small price. The weekly jigsaw puzzle could constitute a solitary or group activity, and would occupy one's time enjoyably for hours. And, of course, a jigsaw puzzle was "recyclable" in that one could break the puzzle up once one had completed it and then pass it on to another family member or friend. Another point to bear in mind that jigsaw puzzle enthusiasts in the Depression discovered what many in our own time are rediscovering — that working on a jigsaw puzzle is a great way to reduce stress. (Daniel McAdam:www.jigsawpuzzle. org/jigsaw-puzzle-history.html)

Puzzles as tools for educational purposes or toys for entertainment or a way to pass the time or a technique for stress relief are four honorable roles that puzzles play in our society and culture. However, when your church or ministry is a collection of disconnected irregularly cut pieces that you are responsible for assembling, the farthest thing from your mind is how entertaining the process will be and what a great way to pass some time, or how much stress will be relieved. In fact, in my ministerial experience those thoughts and emotions are the opposite.

Assembling the disconnected irregularly cut pieces of a church or ministry is not an entertaining, stress-relieving pastime. It is work that requires toiling and struggling. It is not a pastime, yet time will pass in the process. As for stress — it may cause more stress than it relieves.

These are a few reasons I intentionally observed the entertaining, stress-relieving process of solving a jigsaw puzzle to capture principles that are transferable to the jigsaw puzzle of churches and ministries. To do this I took on the role of a metagrobologist — one who studies and solves puzzles.

I even advanced my research beyond my personal study and solving of jigsaw puzzles and included observing others as they solved jigsaw puzzles and interviewed persons about the methods they use to solve jigsaw puzzles. The results of my experience, observation, and research are contained in this work, *Jigsaw Puzzle Leadership.*

Growing up in the pre-electronic video game era of the 1960s and mid-1970s, solving jigsaw puzzles was an activity that required concentration, patience, and persistence. The more pieces the puzzle had, the more difficult and time-consuming putting it together (solving the puzzle) would be. I believe the principles used in the process of solving a jigsaw puzzle are transferable to leadership in ministry or any other organization for that matter.

This book is designed to present jigsaw puzzle-solving principles and apply them to ministry leadership from a biblical perspective. The goal of this writing is to help leaders solve the puzzle of churches and ministries that seem to be in a thousand different disconnected irregularly shaped pieces and are themselves a jigsaw puzzle.

The problems of disconnection are too numerous to mention. However, there are a few that stand head and shoulders above the rest. They include:

- Lack of strength and stability

- Unclear purpose resulting in confusion and frustration

- Distorted identity, when the church or ministry is a collection of disconnected pieces their true identity is distorted. Is it a social service agency? Is it a country club? Is it a business? It's hard to tell what it is when the pieces are disconnected.

- Discouraged members — discouraged because of a lack of strength and stability, unclear purpose, and a distorted identity.

One of the great joys of solving a jigsaw puzzle is placing the last few pieces in place and having a complete picture. It is my desire that you will experience that same joy when, in your church or ministry, you are able to put all the pieces together in their proper places, resulting in strength and stability, clarity of purpose and identity, and members who are encouraged and motivated to engage in and live out the purpose of the church and ministry. Oh, the joy of a solved puzzle!

CHAPTER ONE

SEEING THE BIG PICTURE

While we look at what is;
seeing the Big Picture allows us to see what will be.

Jigsaw puzzles generally come in boxes with a beautiful picture of what the finished product will look like on the top. Then, you open the box and all you see is a collection of disconnected, irregularly shaped pieces. Does this sound like church and ministry? On the outside everything looks beautiful and well put together but once you open it up and get on the inside of the membership and ministry you may discover that there is a collection of disconnected, irregularly shaped members. However, occasionally there may be a few pieces/members that are already properly connected.

> **Jigsaw puzzle:** a puzzle consisting of small irregularly cut pieces that are to be fitted together to form a picture.
>
> — *Webster's Ninth New Collegiate Dictionary*

"Seeing the big picture" is a primary principle of solving a jigsaw puzzle. As a church or ministry leader, seeing the big picture is an indispensable prerequisite. What will the finished product look like? What is the puzzle, church, or ministry supposed to look like? From a biblical perspective, seeing the big picture is "vision" — a divinely inspired mental picture of a preferable future.

Seeing the big picture can be a daunting task. Seeing the big picture involves at least three activities on the part of the leader.

Step Back Far Enough to See the Whole Picture. There is a cultural concept or idiom, a cliché that is applicable here, "Can't see the forest for the trees."

"If you look at things one at a time, you might not realize that a branch of separate 'trees' go together to make a 'forest'. When you are too close to a situation you need to step back and get a little perspective. When you do you will notice there was a whole forest you couldn't see before because you were too close, and focusing on the trees. Simply that you have focused on the many details and have failed to see the overall view, impression, or key point."

(Urban Dictionary)

Seeing the big picture may not be as difficult as it sounds because, again, most leaders are big picture, visionary types. Some leaders are often challenged more to see the individual trees than they are to see the entire forest.

Abraham saw the big picture of a nation, kings, and leaders that God would raise-up from his seed to live in a blessed land (Genesis 12:1-3). Moses saw the big picture of a liberated people, freed from the land of Egypt and the house of bondage, living favorably under the law of God in a blessed land of promise (Exodus 3:1-10). Isaiah saw the big picture of the Messiah's birth and ministry

(Isaiah 7:14; 9:6-7; 42:1-4; 53:1-12; 61:1-3). In each of these cases the big picture (the vision) came from God.

On the cover of the puzzle box is a big picture of what the puzzle is to look like when it is complete. One of the obvious things that the puzzle-solver must notice is the existence of boundaries. Boundaries suggest that, although the picture is big, it does not and cannot include everything.

Big pictures have limitations. Seeing the limits of the big picture is as important as seeing the picture itself. One of the temptations of churches, ministries, organizations, and their leaders is to view themselves as having no limits.

Look Close Enough to be Aware of the Details. Disregarding the details may cause much unnecessary confusion, wasted time, and failure to realize the vision. Most leaders are the big picture "visionary" types who do not always take into consideration the details and myriad connections required to complete the picture and realize the divinely inspired vision. The details, the small stuff, the intricacies of people, programs, and processes should not and must not be ignored.

Attention should also be given to how each detail impacts the whole. It has been said that it is seldom the big things that cause organizations or people to fail, it is the little things. If details challenge or frustrate you, it is important that you have someone on your ministry team who is detail oriented.

You will need to take these individuals by the hand occasionally though, and lead them far enough back to see the big picture. Also, you will need to follow them occasionally into the details. There should be balance between seeing the big picture and having an eye for the details. The details reveal how the pieces fit together.

Someone Else is in Control. The third step in seeing the big picture may not be a step at all but rather an understanding of what the leader brings to the puzzle: *Someone else has predetermined how the pieces fit together.* There are times when working with puzzle pieces that attempts are made to fit pieces together that don't belong together.

The reality is they may look like they fit, you may desire for them to fit, however, how they look and your personal desires are not the determining factors of the pieces' final positions in the puzzle. The manufacturer has predetermined the location for each piece. In the church, ministry leaders and members must understand that God has predetermined the position of each member and how they fit together (more on this in Chapter Three).

Ezekiel's vision of the valley of dry bones is a classic example of seeing the big picture and yet being mindful of the details and aware of God's predetermined will. The vision is given and explained in Ezekiel 37:1-14,

> The hand of the Lord was on me, and he brought me out by the Spirit of the Lord and set me in the middle of a valley; it was full of bones.
>
> He led me back and forth among them, and I saw a great many bones on the floor of the valley, bones that were very dry.
>
> He asked me, "Son of man, can these bones live?" I said, "Sovereign Lord, you alone know."
>
> Then he said to me, "Prophesy to these bones and say to them, 'Dry bones, hear the word of the Lord!

This is what the Sovereign Lord says to these bones: I will make breath enter you, and you will come to life.

I will attach tendons to you and make flesh come upon you and cover you with skin; I will put breath in you, and you will come to life. Then you will know that I am the Lord.'"

So I prophesied as I was commanded. And as I was prophesying, there was a noise, a rattling sound, and the bones came together, bone to bone.

I looked, and tendons and flesh appeared on them and skin covered them, but there was no breath in them.

Then he said to me, "Prophesy to the breath; prophesy, son of man, and say to it, 'This is what the Sovereign Lord says: Come, breath, from the four winds and breathe into these slain, that they may live.'"

So I prophesied as he commanded me, and breath entered them; they came to life and stood up on their feet—a vast army.

Then he said to me: "Son of man, these bones are the people of Israel. They say, 'Our bones are dried up and our hope is gone; we are cut off.'

Therefore prophesy and say to them: 'This is what the Sovereign Lord says: My people, I am going to open your graves and bring you up from them; I will bring you back to the land of Israel.

Then you, my people, will know that I am the Lord, when I open your graves and bring you up from them.

I will put my Spirit in you and you will live, and I will settle you in your own land. Then you will know that I the Lord have spoken, and I have done it, declares the Lord.'"

The text may be outlined as follows:

I. The Revelation of the Details
    Ezekiel 37:1-2

II. The Real Question, "…Can these bones live?"
    Ezekiel 37:3

III. The Revival — God's Will Revealed
     Ezekiel 37:4-6

It must be noted that the preaching of Ezekiel was the instrument that God used to bring the disconnected bones together in their proper places. Never underestimate the power of preaching in puzzling situations. Prophetic preaching, "Thus saith the Lord..." preaching.

IV. The Reveal "...the whole house of Israel..."
Ezekiel 37:11

V. The Reunion — Israel restored to their land.
Ezekiel 37:12-14

With a clear view of the big picture and regular and reasonable attention to details the puzzle solver is well equipped to begin the processes of putting all of the pieces together. I must remind you that churches and ministries do not come in boxes with a picture of what it is to look like printed on the cover. Church and ministry leaders get their big picture (vision) from God. It is a vision that must be captured. Appendix I contains proven strategies for capturing or being captured by God's vision.

CHAPTER TWO

PREPARING TO SOLVE THE PUZZLE

Proper preparation precedes productive performance.

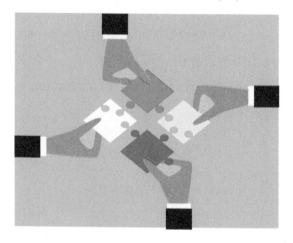

You've got it, a clear picture of what God wants your church or ministry to be and look like! But all you have on hand are a lot of irregularly shaped pieces. Some fit perfectly together, while others are not connected at all. You are at the place and time of having the excitement of seeing the picture on the cover of the puzzle box. However, when you open the box and pour out the pieces, you wonder if these pieces can be put together to make that picture. The short answer is yes, but there are a few valuable steps in the process.

STEP ONE

Preparing the pieces. Place all of the pieces on a smooth level surface. When dealing with the church or a ministry it is important that all of the members be placed on the same level. In the body of Christ, we do not differ in rank, we differ in function. Our function is determined by our shape:

S — Spiritual Gift/s

H — Heart (passion)

A — Ability

P — Personality

E — Experience

(Rick Warren — used by permission)

and the specific ministry to which God has called us.

Church membership longevity, tradition, and local church theology may contribute to a false idea that a member, some members, or a group of members have more prestige, higher rank, or greater significance than others. Not so, according to Paul's instructions to the church at Corinth, the members of our physical bodies (which represent the church body) have been so tempered together by God until those parts that lack honor are given honor and those that are less respectable are given greater respect.

This is the result of God's doing, "… that there may be no division in the body, but that the members may have the same care for one another" (1st Corinthians 12:25). So also is the church the body of Christ.

The smooth level surface must be large enough to accommodate all of the pieces. Sometimes, in ministry we fail to make sufficient room for all of the members and ministries of the church. Making room for members and ministries is expressed in the allocation of funds (church budget), involvement in the planning and implementation of ministry programs and events, designated space in the church facility, allocation of calendar dates and times, and the expectation of collaboration in all things concerning the church and its ministry. It takes all of the pieces to complete the puzzle and it takes all of the members to realize the vision and fulfill the mission of the church. No piece or member should be left behind.

A note about the surface you are working on. It will be extremely helpful and advantageous for the surface to be in a place with excellent lighting and in a location that allows you to move around the surface unencumbered. Are there any dark places in your church or ministry; places where problems go unnoticed, places where the light of the word of God needs to shine?

Do you have the freedom to move in, around, and throughout the entire church and ministry operations and structure? Are there any places or systems that are "off limits"? The puzzle-solver must have full and total access to move in and around all of the parts, pieces and places of the church and its ministries.

STEP TWO

Turn all of the pieces right side up. While doing this, make certain that no piece is covering up or lying on top of another piece. And make sure that no piece is hiding under another piece. The goal is to be able to see all of the pieces and to be engaged with the whole puzzle the entire time. This will take some time, so be patient and realize that some pieces may already be right side up.

As you are turning the upside down pieces right side up, you may discover that some are easier to turn than others. Be persistent. The concepts of turning all of the pieces right side up and placing them in one layer so they may all be seen at once has theological significance for the church and ministry leaders.

During Paul's missionary journeys he traveled extensively preaching the gospel of Jesus Christ. The purpose was to help humanity have a right relationship with God through His Son, Jesus Christ. When Paul and his company arrived at Thessalonica, the unbelieving Jews had a critique of their activities in other places, "These that have turned the world upside down are come here also..." (Acts 17:6 KJV).

Any person or place that is without Christ is already upside down. Now, when that which is already upside down is then turned upside down, it is actually being turned "right side up." No church or ministry should have members who are upside down. All of the members should be right side up. There are several characteristics of a "right side up" member.

"Right side up" members have a proper view and understanding of:

- God and His holiness and that His will is revealed in His Word,

- Themselves and their humanity and utter dependence upon God and their interdependence on one another,

- The relationship between the church and the world;

  ○ *The Church is the light of the world and the salt of the earth* (Matthew 5:13-14).

  ○ *The Church is in the world but not of the world* (John 15:19; Romans 12:1-2).

- The roles and relationships that exist within the church between the scriptural offices (pastor and deacons) and the church members.

- Their responsibility to be fully devoted followers of Christ (mature disciples) engaged in winning the lost and making disciples.

Not only must members be right side up, they should also be on the same level — no big "I's" and little "You's." This is important, so the pastor (and other church leaders) may see all of the members at once. "Keep watch over yourselves and all the flock of which the Holy Spirit has made you overseers…" (Acts 20:28). Pastors must be able to see and oversee all of the members of the local congregation for which they are responsible.

STEP THREE

Identify the key puzzle pieces. There are at least three types of key puzzle pieces.

1. Corner pieces

2. Straight edge pieces

3. Significant pieces

Corner Pieces. As you move around looking closely at each piece, the corner pieces may be a little difficult to identify because there are only four of them. The pieces with a straight edge will be much easier to identify. The significant pieces will stand out because they have the same color or an odd color, or particular pattern based on the big picture.

Straight-edge Pieces. Looking at the picture will help you determine which edge the pieces with the straight edge belong on: the top, bottom, right side or left side. Because they have the straight edge when put together, they will constitute the border or the outer edge of the puzzle. What remains is to fill in the puzzle. Try to complete one edge before moving to another edge, but always set aside pieces with a straight edge because its shape is an indication of its position.

The corner pieces and the straight-edge pieces are key not because they are better, but because of their function.

Significant Pieces. The third key puzzle piece type are those pieces that have the same color, an odd color, or a particular pattern.

I was recently working a jigsaw puzzle that had two butterflies in the big picture — one at the top and one at the bottom of the puzzle. Each had unique colors and patterns on their wings which, upon close observation, made it easy to pick out those pieces from all the rest and put them together outside of the boundaries until enough of the other pieces were in place.

So it is in our churches. There are some members whose uniqueness shapes them for service in specific and particular areas of ministry long before the rest of the puzzle comes together.

The identification of key pieces reminds me of what it must have been like for Nehemiah and the workers as they worked to rebuild the walls of Jerusalem and repair the gates. Many of the stones they used to rebuild the walls were taken from the rubble of the broken down walls. It was painstaking to sift through the rubble in search for the stone with the proper shape to add to the wall.

At one point some of the workers said, "The strength of the bearers of burdens is decayed, and there is much rubbish; so that we are not able to build the wall" (Nehemiah 4:10). With puzzle pieces spread out on the smooth, level surface they resemble rubble as well as the very many dry disconnected bones in Ezekiel's vision.

The most important thing about the puzzle pieces is their shape. If the pieces have no colors, no unique patterns and if there is no big picture, each piece still has its shape. There may be times when God does not readily provide a clear picture of what a local congregation's unique ministry focus should be. The question then becomes, what is a church or ministry to do while it is seeking and waiting on divine revelation?

Remember, every puzzle has corner pieces and straight-edge pieces. Find those and put them together because they will constitute the borders and boundaries for the church and ministry. The boundaries give the church and ministry a context to work in. On the other hand, the word of God is clear about four things that every church and follower of Christ must do:

- Love God — Matthew 22:37

- Love others — Matthew 22:39

- Love one another — John 13:34

- Love enemies — Matthew 5:44

This love motivates praise and worship of God and the study of and obedience to His Word. This love inspires ministry to others in the form of evangelism and social services designed to alleviate human suffering. This love prompts the good works of discipling and edifying one another for their good and God's glory. This love even encourages gracious acts of kindness to one's enemies.

Therefore, long before there is revelation about a church's specific and particular ministry path, there are these love motivating, inspiring, prompting, and encouraging actions that are the hallmarks of every biblically based Christian community of believers.

Shape is so important. The next chapter is dedicated to explaining shape. When church members know their shape, they can be placed in and/or get in where they fit in. The last thing a puzzle solver wants is the right piece in the wrong place, and the last thing a pastor/ministry leader wants is the right member in the wrong place. The goal is "right people in right places."

CHAPTER THREE

RIGHT PEOPLE IN RIGHT PLACES

Right people in wrong places is a formula for frustration.

Few things in life are as uncomfortable and frustrating as being the right person in the wrong place. There are even fewer things in ministry that cause pain, problems, and predicaments more than having the right person in the wrong place.

Over the years I have seen it happen time and time again. A person with little or no leadership or managerial skills is placed in a leadership position. Persons with an introverted personality and limited social skills are placed in the position of a hospitality leader or greeter. Persons with great intellectual ability and verbal communication skills are placed in Bible teaching positions without having the Spiritual gift of teaching.

The late Dr. G. W. Daniel, former president of the Missionary Baptist General Convention of Texas, once said, "A church will call a pastor and the pulpit will still be vacant." That is more than likely the greatest example of the right person being in the wrong place.

One of the goals of jigsaw puzzle leadership is to put right people in right places. In the puzzling process of pastoral and ministry leadership there are several types of people that can be identified: corner piece people, straight-edge piece people, and significant piece people (same color or unique color).

Upon close observation of the three primary puzzle piece types, you will discover some unique characteristics about each type that mirror the people that populate our churches and ministries.

CORNER PIECE PEOPLE

Corner Piece People are Foundational. They can be built upon, they are often the ones that must be in place first or at the start of a project or initiative. They are often the early adopters. In Paul's letter to the Ephesians he lifts the reality of corner piece people in the church.

> Consequently, you are no longer foreigners and aliens, but fellow citizens with God's people and members of God's household, built on the foundation of the apostles and prophets, with Christ Jesus himself as the chief cornerstone.
>
> In him the whole building is joined together and rises to become a holy temple in the Lord. And in him you too are being built to become a dwelling in which God lives by his Spirit.
>
> (Ephesians 2:19-22)

This text clearly shows that the apostles (disciples of Jesus Christ) and prophets were corner piece people providing a foundation upon which the household of God could be built — a household that has Jesus Himself as the chief cornerstone.

As builders (puzzle solvers) pastors and church leaders must be wise master builders (puzzle solvers) as was Paul — fully understanding that whatever is assembled, put together, or built as it relates to the church and ministry must have Jesus Christ as the foundation. Paul states,

> By the grace God has given me, I laid a foundation as an expert builder, and someone else is building on it.
>
> But each one should be careful how he builds. For no one can lay any foundation other than the one already laid, which is Jesus Christ.
>
> (1 Corinthians 3:10-11)

The shape of the corner pieces enables them to have at least two distinct functions in the church or ministry. First, they function as a stopping point. Corners are stopping points. They insure that healthy boundaries and limitations are firmly in place. Corner piece people keep others from going too far.

My father, Reverend A. L. Dew, who in the descriptive words of Gardner Taylor, "Now sleeps the long sleep of death" used to say, "There is such a thing as going too far." He would also say, "You can overdo a thing."

The wisdom writer of Proverb 29:18 says, "Where there is no prophecy, the people cast off restraint..."

Where there are no corner pieces, there are no stopping points and churches and ministries and their members are unrestrained — lacking sufficient boundaries to keep them in the will of God. Corner piece people are stopping points.

The second unique function of corner piece people is their ability to inspire a change in direction. Corners are places where turns can be made. From time to time churches and ministries need to shift their focus and change the direction of their ministry. There are several factors that contribute to a corner piece saying, "Stop and change directions." Some of the factors include:

- Changes in the ministry context

- Population shifts in the community

- Life cycle of programs and events

- Improved technology and the use thereof
- The needs of the church and community
- The guiding direction of the Holy Spirit

There are several places in scripture where corner piece people changed the direction and focus of their ministry and the ministry of others.

- *Jesus goes through Samaria, a place previously avoided.* John 4:3-4

- *Peter changes directions of his ministry to include Gentiles.* Acts 11:1-9

- *Paul and his missionary team were prevented from going where they desired to go, however, after receiving a vision they changed their direction.* Acts 16:6-10

- *Apollos changed the focus of his preaching after an encounter with the corner piece couple Aquila and Priscilla.* Acts 18:24-26

Every church and ministry needs the stopping influence and the directional change initiation of corner piece people. It must also be noted that in a puzzle there are only four corner pieces. In churches and ministries you will not find many corner people — only a few who are shaped to set limits and motivate change. Find them, place them, appreciate and celebrate them. Above all allow their shape to influence the church and ministry.

STRAIGHT-EDGE PIECE PEOPLE

Straight-Edge Piece People have three sides that are varied and one side that is straight. This particular shape is an indication of at least two characteristics. First, straight-edge people are predictable. Because one side is straight this is the primary indicator that their position is on the outer edge of the church or ministry. This particular capacity proves their ability to go to the edge, be on the edge, and stay on the edge.

The edge can be the cutting edge — the place where trailblazers thrive, cutting new paths and finding new routes. At times they, in partnership with God, are able to make a way where there is no way. The cutting edge utilizes a compass and not a map. A map is a constant reminder that someone has already traveled that way. While traveling (serving and ministering) with a compass allows one to stay on course as a new path is being cut.

The edge is not for everyone, the edge can be risky. The edge can be scary. However, the edge is the place where the miraculous is most often experienced.

The edge can also be the creative edge. Creating new approaches, methods, means, and ministries to fulfill the great commission — "make disciples" and the great commandment — "love God and others" with a great commitment. Every church and ministry needs members who are out on the edge. However, the straight edge pieces are still connected to the other pieces.

The second characteristic of straight edge people is their dependability. Because one of their sides is straight, they can be counted on, relied upon, and depended on to take a particular position in the church or ministry. Their shape dictates their service.

These are the straight-shooting, no-nonsense, tell-it-like-it-is individuals. These are the "truth tellers" in the ministry even when the truth hurts. Paul challenged the Galatians with the truth and based upon their response to him and the truth he shared with them he asked, "Am I become your enemy because I tell you the truth" (Galatians 4:16)?

The truth is not always received with joy and gladness but it must always be spoken in love with a goal of making things better.

Finding and connecting the straight-edge pieces to the corner pieces, and then to one another will allow you to see the outline of the church and ministry. Once the outer edges are in place, all that remains is filling in the puzzle with the other pieces.

Throughout this process the puzzle-solver must keep the big picture in view and refer to it often. Even the people (pieces) need to be reminded often of what the finished picture will look like. Each piece must get in where they fit in — right people in right places. Looking at the big picture, you will see areas that are the same color.

SAME COLOR PEOPLE

Looking at the three sample puzzle pictures you can immediately see sections and segments of each puzzle that are one color. This lets you know that there are several of these color pieces that make up that part of the puzzle.

To aid you in solving the puzzle, gather the the same color pieces together. When describing a puzzle, I use color literally, but for the church and ministry it is used figuratively. The figurative use of color represents a person's personality and passions.

There are several personality tests that use color to represent a particular personality type. One such test was developed by Taylor Hartman, PhD. Hartman uses four primary colors which are described in the following way:

RED

Motive [Power]: Reds are the power wielders. Power: the ability to move from point A to point B and get things done. This is what motivates and drives these people. They bring great gifts of vision and leadership and generally are responsible, decisive, proactive and assertive.

BLUE

Motive [Intimacy]: Blues are the do-gooders. Intimacy: connecting, creating quality relationships and having purpose is what motivates and drives these people. They bring great gifts of quality and service and are generally loyal, sincere, and thoughtful.

WHITE

Motive [Peace]: Whites are the peacekeepers. Peace: the ability to stay calm and balanced even in the midst of conflict is what motivates and drives these people. They bring great gifts of clarity and tolerance and are generally kind, adaptable, and good listeners.

YELLOW

Motive [Fun]: Yellows are the fun-lovers. Fun: the joy of living life in the moment is what motivates and drives these people. They bring great gifts of enthusiasm and optimism and are generally charismatic, spontaneous, and sociable.

Assembling pieces and people according to their common color will contribute to your ability to solve the puzzle. It must be noted that the way color works is when separated, yet functioning interdepen-

dently, various colors may form a beautiful rainbow. On the other hand, when all the colors are mixed together the result is the color black. Black has its place but the picture of your puzzle, church or ministry should not be the one color black.

Paul teaches that the church is not one member (color or personality) but many (1 Corinthians 12:4). In every puzzle, church or ministry there are common reoccurring colors and there are rare, unique, and unusual colors. These must also be identified.

UNIQUE COLOR PEOPLE

Not long ago, I was working a puzzle that was a picture of a tiger and a tiger cub. The pieces of the puzzle that contained the unique colors were the pieces that formed the eyes of the tigers. There were approximately 6-8 pieces that connected to form each of the four eyes.

At first glance, it was difficult to pick out the pieces that formed the eyes. But the more I looked at the picture on the box (attention to details) the more my mind was able to focus the search, thereby making the search easier.

The leader/puzzle solver must have a balanced perspective of both the disconnected, irregularly shaped pieces (church/ministry members) and the final outcome (God's vision) as it is depicted on the cover of the puzzle box. To be overly focused on the one and not the other is unhealthy.

If you only focus on the pieces, you will become frustrated, confused, and puzzled. Only focusing on the picture of the future may place you in the position to be so heavenly minded that you are of little or no earthly good.

Each puzzle piece type has its own special function in the puzzle. The corner pieces are foundational and provide stopping points and turning points. The straight edge pieces are made for the edge. They are predictable and reliable. The majority of the pieces have common colors. Grouping them according to their color type will aid in solving the puzzle.

Finally, the unique pieces are the rare pieces that, when connected, create an odd shape or color within the puzzle. Warning: even though the pieces may share aspects of their shape, size, and color — no two pieces are exactly the same.

Again, I use by permission, Rick Warren's book, *Purpose Driven Life*, published in 2002. In the book, Warren presents five purposes for life and living. One of those purposes is "Shaped for Service." Warren uses the acronym S.H.A.P.E. to describe and define the focus that forges a person's shape. *Christian Book Summaries,*

Volume 2, Issue 23 offers the following summary of Warren's S.H.A.P.E.:

S is for Spiritual Gifts. God has given every believer certain divinely empowered abilities to build up His body. We are not to focus on the gifts we do not have but on using those that God has given us.

H is for Heart. God has given each of us a unique emotional "heartbeat" that beats more passionately for some things than for others. Since God wants you to serve Him with your whole heart, these passions can be a clue as to your place of service.

A is for Abilities. The average person has 500 to 700 different skills and abilities. Some are inborn, others acquired. Since they come from God, they are just as important, just as spiritual, as your spiritual gifts.

P is for Personality. God loves variety, and He uses all types of personalities and temperaments. It should feel good to do what God made you to do, and this will help you to determine where and how you should serve.

E is for Experiences. Experiences from your family, education, vocation, spiritual walk, ministry, and personal difficulties will help define your place of service. The painful experiences, which we would rather forget, are perhaps the most telling.

In the appendix you will find tools that are designed to help a person discover their spiritual gift/s and their personality type.

CHAPTER FOUR

PUTTING ALL THE PIECES TOGETHER

The places where connections happen are the places of our greatest possibilities.

Jigsaw Puzzle Leadership consists of four principles:

1. SEEING THE BIG PICTURE

This involves capturing God's vision for the future as it is described in Appendix I.

A. Study the Scriptures

B. Solitude and silence

C. Fasting and prayer

D. Observation of current congregational and community felt needs

Seeing the Big Picture means understanding that God is calling and guiding how and where each member fits in the church and ministry.

2. PREPARING THE PIECES

A. Place all the pieces on the same level

B. Turn all the pieces right side up

C. Make room to move in and around all of the pieces

3. IDENTIFYING THE KEY PIECES

A. Corner Pieces/People

B. Straight-Edge Pieces/People

C. Same Color Pieces/People

D. Unique Color Pieces/People

4. PUTTING ALL THE PIECES TOGETHER: RIGHT PEOPLE IN RIGHT PLACES

Place people where they fit. Encourage people to get in where they fit in. Some people look at this process as trial and error. Not so, it is trial and trial, and trial, etc... until the person is in his or her proper place.

The fact that they have been added to the church or ministry indicates there is a special or unique place for them to thrive as well as contribute to the health and wellbeing of the body. Consider Judges 7:21, "And they stood every man in his place round about the camp..." When the right people are in the right places, there is no force that cannot be overcome.

The fourth principle: "Putting all the pieces together: Right People In Right Places" is the focus of this concluding chapter.

At this point in the process of solving the puzzle, you will have a full view of the Big Picture, having captured God's vision for the future of your church or ministry. Putting all of the pieces together involves clearly communicating the vision — the divinely inspired picture of a preferable future — to the leaders and members of the church or ministry.

Communicating the vision is more than just announcing to them what it is or telling them what you have received from the Lord. Communicating the vision is sharing it with such simplicity and clarity that the leaders and members "see it" themselves. "Seeing it" implies understanding it, grasping the value and importance of it, and agreeing with the future conditions that will exist when the vision is realized.

One great mistake leaders often make is believing that after one "vision-casting session" everyone "sees it." It has been my experience that lay-leaders and church members seldom see the vision the first two or three times it is presented to them.

Therefore, the process of communicating the vision may require one-on-one sessions with lay-leaders followed by small group vision-casting sessions with lay-leaders then a series of vision-casting sessions with the membership at large. The vision-casting sessions with the membership at large may be in the form of a series of sermons or Bible study lessons or both.

When using these methods to cast vision, it is important that the hearers and students are informed that the sermons and lessons are specifically designed to help everyone "see" what God is calling the church or ministry to be and/or do.

Once the greater portion of the lay-leaders and members "see" the vision, the next step is to gain "buy-in." Sometimes, when lay-leaders and members see the vision, they see it as the pastor's vision. I have even heard people in their prayers ask God to bless the "Pastor's vision."

Not much will happen in the realization of the vision until the lay-leaders and members "buy-in" to the vision. Whoever "buys-in" becomes an owner of the vision. Ownership means responsibility — responsibility to bring the vision to reality. The vision ceases to be the "Pastor's vision and becomes "our vision."

There is an occasion in scripture when there was an immediate "buy-in" to a vision. "And a vision appeared to Paul in the night; There stood a man of Macedonia, and prayed him, saying. 'Come over into Macedonia, and help us.' And after he had seen the vision, immediately we endeavored to go into Macedonia, assuredly gathering that the Lord had called us for to preach the gospel unto them" (Acts 16:9-10 KJV).

From my experience and perspective this is a miracle. "…[A]fter he had seen the vision, immediately we endeavored to go…" seldom is there a "…immediately we…" but with God all things are possible. Paul's companions interpreted the vision he had seen as God's call to all of them.

So it is with the vision God gives to a pastor, the vision is to the pastor but it is for the church. The sooner the people "see it" and "buy-in" to it the sooner the vision will be realized.

After capturing and buying into the vision, it is important that members know or discover their shape, color, and uniqueness. It is only when members know, accept and are operating effectively in their area/s of giftedness that God's vision for the church or ministry can and will be realized. It is one's shape that determines where and how to fit into the puzzle that is the church.

Members must be encouraged to get in where they fit in. A forced fit is a misfit. There are times when people are shaped for a certain ministry but they resist embracing it. These are times when they must let it be so, as in the case of John the Baptist. "The cam Jesus from Galilee to the Jordan to be baptized by John. But John tried to deter him saying, 'I need to be baptized by you and do you come to me?' Jesus replied, 'Let it be so now: it is proper for us to do this to fulfill all righteousness.' Then John consented." (Matthew 3:13-15)

When people serve in the areas for which they are shaped, it fulfills righteousness, it fulfills God's will for them and it adds value to the church and ministry. Jesus himself reached a place where he struggled with God's will for his life yet we hear him say, "…not what I will, but what you will" (Mark 14:36).

Think it not strange when people try to do things for which they are not shaped or when they attempt to avoid things for which they are shaped. These are the times that we must remind them of the Big Picture and how it will not be complete as long as they are not in their proper place. We must also remind them that no one else is shaped for their place but them.

Much has been said about "S.H.A.P.E.". I must also share the reality that during the course of one's journey with Jesus and involvement in ministry, it is not unusual for them to experience a change in their shape. In fact, a person seldom maintains their original shape during the course of their entire ministry. Don't be amazed if and when God, whose workmanship we are, decides to change our shape so our place in the puzzle may also change.

David was shaped to shepherd sheep, but God changed his shape to rule Israel. Joseph, whose childhood dreams informed him that he was shaped for greatness, was first shaped to serve in Potiphar's house, then shaped to serve in prison; and finally, he was shaped to be second in command in all of Egypt. No doubt God used Potiphar and prison to shape Joseph.

In my own life and times, I have witnessed shape changes in the lives of others. Changing from Youth Pastor to Senior Pastor and from Senior Pastor to an Encourager, etc...

When a person is being placed in a ministry position, or when a person is getting in where they fit in, it should be in response to a sense of God's call. When there is a missing puzzle piece and there is a member who is shaped for that place, I encourage them to pray and seek God's leading before they move into a ministry position.

It is my conviction that when a person is serving out of a sense of calling, their level of commitment is greater than it would be under any other circumstances. As pastors and ministry leaders we must allow for trial and trail, and trial, permitting people to serve in a variety of places until they find the place that fits best.

When they are trying a ministry position, everyone in that ministry needs to know that this is a trial. Once a person finds the place that fits, encourage them to get in where they fit in. Having all of the people in the places where they fit means that the puzzle has been solved, and the vision has been realized. Praise the Lord!!!

CAPTURING GOD'S VISION FOR THE FUTURE

"Where there is no vision, the people perish."

~Proverb 29:18

When I embarked on this journey of discovery, I believed that I would find something new and profound that would inform those who are in pursuit of God's Vision for the Future, the big picture for the local church. What I encountered was stated best by

Patrick Lencion at the 2012 Willow Creek Association's Global Leadership Summit, "People need to be reminded of what they already know more than they need to be taught something new."

This appendix is the documentation of the many reminders that I was given while trying to discover how to capture God's vision for the future. I must admit that there were a few new lessons along the way, but for the most part I found myself digging the old wells. The presentation of this information will be in four parts:

- Part One — Divine Revelation in the Old Testament

- Part Two — Divine Revelation and the Early Church

- Part Three— Divine Revelation Through Solitude and Silence

- Part Four — Divine Revelation by Personal Pursuit

PART ONE: Divine Revelation in the Old Testament

The Old Testament is an enormous body of work. It would do well to narrow the focus to a few individuals who were able to lead effectively because of the knowledge and clear picture they had about the future. In an interview with Dr. Jason Gile, on August 7, 2012, he identified four leadership roles in the Old Testament that must be noted: (1) Kings; (2) Judges; (3) Priests; (4) Prophets. To this list I add the Patriarchs and the persons Moses and Joshua.

Dr. Gile shared that the prophetic role is the role that best addresses the topic of capturing God's vision for the future. Some of the personalities that fulfilled that role include Isaiah, Ezekiel, Jeremiah, David, and Samuel. In addition to these, there were King David, King Solomon, and the patriarchs Abraham, Isaac, and Jacob. Each of these personalities were privileged to receive from God insight into the future, a view of the big picture.

The most significant idea that came out of my interview with Dr. Gile is that God is the initiator of the prophetic. Among the personalities listed above there are four that stand out. The primary information they received about the future came to them in what is called the "call narrative." The call narrative is a type of form criticism that enabled scholars to identify this specific genre.

There are three distinctive elements that appear regularly in the stories of various individuals. "Yahweh calls the person to perform a task (commission); the person expresses their unworthiness or inability (concern); Yahweh gives the person reassurance (comfort)."[1]

Abraham's call is recorded in Genesis 12:1-5 (KJV),

> Now the LORD had said unto Abram, Get thee out of thy country, and from thy kindred, and from thy father's house, unto a land that I will shew thee:
>
> And I will make of thee a great nation, and I will bless thee, and make thy name great; and thou shalt be a blessing: And I will bless them that bless thee, and curse him that curseth thee: and in thee shall all families of the earth be blessed.
>
> So Abram departed, as the LORD had spoken unto him; and Lot went with him: and Abram was seventy and five years old when he departed out of Haran.
>
> And Abram took Sarai his wife, and Lot his brother's son, and all their substance

that they had gathered, and the souls that they had gotten in Haran; and they went forth to go into the land of Canaan; and into the land of Canaan they came.

Abraham's big picture was "a great nation."

It must be noted that this account does not record any dialogue between Abraham (Abram) and God. Just a command and a promise followed by Abraham's obedience. Abraham would not have left home when he did, the way he did, if he had not seen the big picture.

Even though this call is to an individual it is or was inclusive of what would be the nation of Israel. "Gonzalez suggests that the call of Abraham is not so much that of an individual as the call of a nation: 'If there was at one time a personal experience, it was stripped of its personal significance in the pre-literary stages of history, and thus became meaningful for everyone.'"[2]

The call narrative of Moses is one of the most detailed of the call narratives recorded in scripture. It is recorded in Exodus chapters 3 and 4, "…Where Moses voices a series of five questions or objections to God, all expressing his hesitancy to accept the task of leading God's people out of Egypt: 'Who am I that I should go' (3:11);

'What shall I say to them?'; 'I am slow of speech' (4:10); 'Send someone else' (4:13). 'I will be with you.'"[3] There are at least five elements in the call narrative of Moses: (1) confrontation; (2) commission; (3) objections; (4) assurance; (5) sign.

It must be noted that there was nothing that Moses did to gain or obtain knowledge of what God was going to do in the lives of the Hebrew people. God initiated the contact and the communication that contained big picture revelation and inspiration for Moses' participation.

> Significantly, God is given a voice but no shape or form in the biblical account of the theophany on Mount Horeb. The men and women who contributed the oldest strands of narrative to the biblical tapestry understood God to be a distinctly camera-shy deity, and the first of the Ten Commandments would forbid the making of His image. So the first encounter between God and Moses in the Bible is left intentionally vague. Indeed, the biblical account of what happened when Moses found himself in conversation with God — an experience that we might imagine to be awe-inspiring and blood-shaking — is striking only in its restraint and understate-

ment. That God chose to manifest Himself in something so ordinary as a bush — 'a familiar sight in the pasture lands,' as one Bible scholar observes — seems a humble gesture for the King of the Universe.[4]

So often is the case that God makes adjustments to Himself in order to communicate with men rather than men making adjustments to encounter and/or hear from God.

The narrative of Samuel's call is another example of God taking the initiative in communicating big picture divine revelation as it is recorded in 1 Samuel 3:1-10. The key verse in the narrative is 1 Samuel 3:7, "Now Samuel did not yet know the Lord, neither was the Word of the Lord yet revealed unto him (KJV)."

In His encounter with Samuel, God not only reveals His vision for the future of Eli and Eli's house, but He also revealed Himself to Samuel. "And the Lord appeared again in Shiloh for the Lord revealed Himself to Samuel in Shiloh by the Word of the Lord (1st Samuel 3:21 KJV)."

The only thing that Samuel did to capture God's vision for the future was to make himself available to hear God once he knew that God was speaking to him. He did nothing to motivate God to speak to him. In fact, when he first heard God's voice he laid down to sleep and actually thought it was Eli calling him.

The beauty of the narrative is God's consistent calling until both Eli and Samuel realized that God was speaking. God was deliberate in His desire to capture Samuel's attention in order to communicate with him as opposed to Samuel doing something to capture God's vision.

> It is possible that this emphasis on the divine activity of God reveals a more priestly perspective, but this connection is far from certain. What seems more certain is that this emphasis on the side of God with little or no response from the person suggests a perspective that wants to emphasize leadership as grounded in God's revelatory activity in the world. That is, leadership of God's people is a response to an understanding of God as He reveals Himself to human beings. The use of this form of the commissioning narrative would emphasize that God is active in the world, that He is at work in unfolding historical events, and that leadership of God's people must be grounded in an understanding of that activity of God in the world.[5]

Isaiah's call narrative is recorded in Isaiah 6:1-13. Carlo Carretto says,

> God's call is mysterious; it comes in the darkness of faith. It is so fine, so subtle, that it is only with the deepest silence within us that we can hear it. And yet nothing is so decisive and overpowering for a man or woman on this earth, nothing surer or stronger. This call is uninterrupted: God is always calling us. But there are distinctive moments in this call of His, moments which leave a permanent mark on us moments which we never forget.[6]

These are moments when we see the big picture.

Such was the case with Isaiah. It was, "In the year that King Uzziah died I saw the Lord." (Isaiah 6:1 KJV) This was an encounter that Isaiah would never forget. His experience included both divine and human revelation as well as commissioning into service. God revealed the awesome holiness of His divinity which, in turn, caused Isaiah to see the frail, faulty incompletion of his humanity and the humanity of those around him.

As an act of gracious redemption Isaiah is purged and his sins are taken away then he hears the question from God, "Whom shall I send, and who will go for us?" To which Isaiah responds, "Here am I; send me (Isaiah 6:8)." It is at this point in the call narrative that God makes plain Isaiah's assignment as well as His plans for the future of the Hebrew people.

The common quality in each of these call narratives and the revelation of future events contained within them is that God was the initiator. There was nothing done on the part of the recipients that contributed to their ability to capture God's vision for the future. "God, who at sundry times and in divers manners spoke in time past unto the fathers... (Hebrews 1:1)." "This is the Lord's doing; it is marvelous in our eyes (Psalm 118:23)." We capture God's vision when He reveals it to us.

PART TWO: Divine Revelation and the Early Church

The focus of this section is the second century until the end of the reign of Constantine in 337. The majority of the content of this section comes from an interview with Dr. Sam Hamstra on July 27, 2012. Our conversation centered around the methods used by the early church fathers to capture God's vision for the future.

At the outset Hamstra shared that the book of Revelation was the primary source of inspiration and information that the early church fathers used to form their understanding of the future. In consideration of that position three of the opening verses of the book of Revelation should be considered. Revelation 1:1, "The Revelation of Jesus Christ, which God gave unto Him, to show unto His servants things which must shortly come to pass; and he sent and signified it by his angel unto his servant John."

This book contains things which must shortly come to pass. When the early church fathers desired to know what God had in store for them they studied the writing of John. The second verse that should be considered is Revelation 1:10, "I was in the Spirit on the Lord's day…" God's vision of the future was given to John. It came to him while he was in the Spirit. Paul says to Timothy in 2 Timothy 3:16, "All scripture is given by inspiration of God…"

From these two scriptures it must be noted that there can be no revelation apart from the activity of God and the Holy Spirit.

The third key opening verse of the book of Revelation is 1:19. This particular verse gives an outline of the contents of the book, "Write the things which thou hast seen, and the things which are, and the things which shall be hereafter." Warren Wiersbe, in his book, *Expository Outlines of the New Testament,* offers the following suggested outline of the book of Revelation.

1. The Things Which Thou Hast Seen (1)

    A. John's vision of the glorified Christ as King-Priest

2. The Things Which Are (2-3)

    A. The seven churches reveal the condition of God's people.

3. The Things Which Shall Be Hereafter (4-22)

    A. The rapture of the church (4-5)

        1. John is caught up

        2. The Lamb takes the throne

    B. The tribulation of seven years (6-19)

        1. First half of the tribulation (6-9)

        2. Middle of the tribulation (10-14)

3. Last half of the tribulation (15-19)

C. The millennial kingdom of Christ (20)

D. The new heavens and earth (21-22)"

The primary interest of the early church fathers was the physical return of Christ and the fulfilling culmination of the church. The contributing factor of this particular interest was the persecution that the church was facing in the decades prior to the rise of Constantine.

According to Hamstra, more often than not one's cultural context helps shape their vision of the future. A church persecuted is drawn to messages and prophesies of deliverance, defeat of enemies, triumphant victory, and lasting peace. These are the messages of the book of Revelation.

The early church fathers had enough historical data, experience, and scriptures to engage in what could be called forecasting. In fact capturing God's vision for the future may come primarily from forecasting. Forecasting is a concept that involves consideration of the current times using wisdom, insight, systems analysis, and discernment to predict what would Among the early church fathers who depended upon scripture to inform their understanding of the future are Irenaeus, Tertullian, and Origen.

> Irenaeus helps the early church to realize both the internal nature of Scripture and the ecclesiological authority of Scripture. Internally, Scripture is seen as true and a measure of truth, and the Old and New Testaments cohere and evidence each other. This view of Scripture translates to an exegesis that is constant and includes both testaments. Externally, his use of the writing of the apostles evidences a notion of canonicity and helps to delineate the use of particular texts in the early Christian West.
>
> Perhaps the most impressive feature about Irenaeus is his employment of the teaching of Jesus and the church as a standard for belief for all churches throughout the world.[7]

Tertullian's contribution was significant to both the church and the world. Tertullian explained to pagans what divine revelation was and how it could be perceived. He mentioned both the written word of Scripture, explaining its origin, and also the testimony of nature:

In order that we might acquire a fuller and more authoritative knowledge both of himself and of his counsels and will, God has added a written revelation for the benefit of everyone whose heart is set on seeking Him, so that by seeking he may find and by finding believe, and by believing obey. From the first, He sent messengers into the world — men whose stainless righteousness made them worthy to know the Most High, and to reveal Him — men abundantly endowed with the Holy Spirit, that they might proclaim that there is only one God, who made all things, who formed man from the dust of the ground — for He is the true Prometheus who put order into the world by arranging the seasons and their course. These have further set before us the proofs He has given of His majesty in His judgements by floods and fires, the rules appointed by Him for securing His favour, as well as the retribution in store. We too, used to laugh at these things. We are of your stock and nature, for men are made, not born, Christians. The preachers of whom we have spoken are called prophets, from the office which belongs to them of predicting the future. Their words, along with the miracles which they performed in order for men to have faith in their divine authority, are recorded in the literary treasures which they have left us, and which are open to all.[8]

Finally, Brady states Origen's belief that the Scriptures are the source of truth and life.

Origen's greatest work was his theological tome *On First Principles*. In it he describes the elemental or foundational truths by which Christian doctrine must be pursued. Written between 220 and 230 while Origen was in his prime at Alexandria, the work starkly reveals the cosmic scope of his thought. The following selection from the preface is critical for understanding Origen's interpretative method, for it highlights the Christocentric nature of scriptural exegesis:

All who believe and are convinced that grace and truth came by Jesus Christ, and who know Christ to be the truth (in accordance with His own saying, 'I am the truth') derive the knowledge which calls men to lead a good and blessed life from no other source but the very words and teaching of Christ. By the words of Christ we do not mean only those which formed His teaching when He was made man and dwelt in the flesh, since even before that Christ the Word of God was in Moses and the prophets. For without the Word of God how could they have prophesied about Christ? In proof of which we should not find it difficult to show from the divine scriptures how Moses or the prophets were filled with the spirit of Christ in all their words and deeds, were we not anxious to confine the present work within the briefest possible limits. I count it sufficient, therefore, to quote this one testimony of Paul, taken from the epistle he writes to the Hebrews, where he speaks as follows: 'By faith Moses, when he was grown up, refused to be called the son of Pharaoh's daughter, choosing rather to suffer affliction with the people of God than to enjoy the pleasures of sin for a season, accounting the reproach of Christ greater riches than the treasures of Egypt.' And as for the fact that Christ spoke in the apostles after His ascension into heaven, this is shown by Paul in the following passage: 'Or do ye seek a proof of Him that speaketh in me, that is, Christ.'[9]

All who have come since the time of the early church fathers would do well to begin with scripture as the starting point for capturing God's vision of the future.

PART THREE: Divine Revelation Through Solitude and Silence

This section of capturing God's vision for the future investigates St. Benedict and his Rule for the monastic life as a contributing factor in capturing God's vision for the future. From my interview with Dr. Parker on July 18, 2012 I was given the following information about St. Benedict:

> "Benedict (c. 480-547) was born around the year 480 in the Umbrian province of Nursia in Italy after the fall of Rome in A.D. 410 and the official end of the Western empire in 476. It was a dangerous and turbulent time. In his biography of St. Benedict, Pope Gregory the Great (590-604) described Benedict's family as one of high station. He was sent to Rome but soon abandoned his studies, leaving the city that he felt was too corrupt. Several years later he went to an area near the town of Subiaco where he lived as a hermit in a hill side cave for three years. There

he was 'discovered' by others who recognized his holiness and wisdom. He founded the monastery of Subiaco, which still exist today, along with eleven other monasteries on the hillside. Benedict left the area when a jealous local priest attempted to poison him through the gift of tainted blessed bread! Benedict then traveled to Monte Cassino in the imposing mountains of the central Italian Apennines where he formed a new community and remained there for the rest of his life. Benedict had a sister, Scholastica, who had established herself nearby with her own community of nuns. It was said that they met together once a year. Benedict died in 547. Forty years after his death the monastery was destroyed by the Lombards. Today the relics of St. Benedict may be found at the Abbey of St. Benoitsur-Loire in France.

Benedict is most known for the creation of a monastic rule. He wrote this rule for the monks of his own monastery at Monte Cassion, having no thought of establishing a monastic rule that would be adopted by others. Yet, within a century or two after his death in 547, Benedict had become the patriarch of Western monasticism and his Rule the most influential in the Western Church. By the Middle Ages, most of the monasteries of the West followed his Rule, as many do this day. Benedict would be astounded indeed to know that fifteen centuries later you and I would look at his Rule for guidance in our own lives.

Through his Rule Benedict reveals wisdom and understanding along with a very astute knowledge of human behavior. But most of all, the Rule reveals Benedict's love for his brothers, his love of Christ and his desire that his monks, and us by extension, follow Christ's way to eternal life."

The first word in the prologue of the Rule is, "listen." Esther de Waal in her book, *Seeking God: The Way of St. Benedict* says, "From the start the disciple's goal is to hear keenly and sensitively that word of God which is not only message but event and encounter."

This kind of listening is enhanced by solitude and silence. "St. Benedict's understanding of listening falls into this order; it is the listening of the whole person, of body as well as intellect and it requires love as well as cerebral assent. And it also involves mindfulness — an awareness which turns listening from a cerebral activity into a living response."

The listening of which St. Benedict speaks is listening to the Word of God. His Word is His will. His desires for the future are in His Word. He is His Word. Capturing His Word through listening means capturing Him and all that He has, intends, and wills for the present and the future.

"Faith comes by hearing and hearing by the Word of God." (Romans 10:17) "Now faith is the substance of things hoped for, the evidence of things not seen." (Hebrews 11:1) Through listening to the Word of God one's faith is developed and it is that faith that brings the future into the present.

Benedict's teaching on encountering God is threefold.

1. **God is present where you are.**

    All too often people go off somewhere to find or experience God when He is everywhere. The challenge of the seeker is to open up to the "very presence" of God.

2. **The experience is often gentle.**

    This is reminiscent of Elijah's experience recorded in 1 Kings 19:11-12,

"And he said. 'Go forth and stand upon the mount before the Lord.' And behold, the Lord passed by, and a great and strong wind rent the mountains, and brake in pieces the rocks before the Lord; but the Lord was not in the wind: and after the wind an earthquake; but the Lord was not in the earthquake: and after the earthquake a fire. But the Lord was not in the fire: and after the fire a still small voice."

God was in the still small voice. If care is not taken it is possible for God to pass by unnoticed. It is interesting to note that Benedict emphasizes listening and God shows up in a still small voice. John 1:1 records, "In the beginning was the Word, and the Word was with God, and the Word was God."

3. It can happen every day.

This is the blessing of a personal relationship with God through Jesus Christ. There is daily communion and fellowship. It is not reserved for a special day, a holiday, or a holy day. An encounter with God can happen every day. There may be days when the encounter is more intense than others. In those cases care must be taken not to esteem the day but rather the encounter because the encounter can happen every day.

PART FOUR: Divine Revelation By Personal Pursuit

This final section is the compilation and summary of responses to four questions regarding capturing God's vision for the future. The respondents are pastors from a variety of backgrounds and experiences.

Question: What steps do you take to discover God's will for the future of the church you are serving?

Answers:

1. First I consult with God through prayer and ask Him for guidance and direction. I think through the ideas, concepts, and vision that God has given. I develop clear and detailed schematic of the vision that God gave and discuss it with the ministerial leadership, trustees, and deacons. I get "buy-in" with the leadership team in developing mission, purpose, biblical and contemporaneous relevance, importance, and church direction specificity.

2. One of the main steps that I take is prayer — seeking God's will and asking Him what will He have me to do as a pastor in leading His people.

3. I cannot say that I have a clear methodology in this regard, but I would point to the following factors:

    (1) Personal prayer and though asking the Holy Spirit to enlighten me as I seek direction for the church;

    (2) Personal observation and research: What's going on in the church? What's going on in the community? What are the church's strengths and weaknesses? Is the church already gifted to meet needs in the community?

    (3) Discussion and prayer with church leaders. I am of the persuasion that the Holy Spirit can speak to and through others in the body of Christ. I look for consensus and passion around a specific ministry focus from those who are going to help lead the church into its future.

4. My first step would be to go to God in prayer asking that He reveal His will in respect to the com-

munity in which the church exists. I was taught to exegete not only the community, but the congregation. The small church where I am blessed to pastor is mostly 60% senior. The closing prayer before the benediction is augmented by the congregation and I saying, "Lord send us help."

I believe that no matter what my visions are, unless they are part of the will of God for the church it can't work. That means listening for God to speak not only to me, but to someone else also.

5. God's will is revealed in His Word. The biblical events give us insight into His plans and are therefore known to have significance for the future of the church.

6. I seek God's will for the future of the church through fasting and fervent prayer for His guidance for the development of the church body. The primary goal is to develop the church body spiritually — to prepare individual souls for individual transitioning before God through Christ Jesus. I solicit auxiliaries of the church to support

the membership physically through various outreach programs.

7. At the end of each calendar year I try to spend a committed time in prayer, fasting, and seeking the Lord's face for direction and an annual focus or ministry theme. Sometimes, I will go off on a personal 2-3 day retreat with my Bible, notepad, and a few books. After this time of consecration, we have a 3-day Strategic Planning meeting at which myself and my Executive Council get together to put an implementation plan in place.

   As I share with them, we create detailed strategies to in place that will help us accomplish the goal. On our final day of meeting, we go back and reduce the plan, if necessary, to fit our capacity and resources. Lastly we will assign ministry leaders ownership to the components of the plan that they will be responsible for overseeing.

Question: What tools do you give to your ministry leaders or how do you equip them to capture God's will for their respective ministries?

Answers:

1. I provide an annual series on "Identification of Spiritual Gifts" and "Church Operations in the Light of Unity." I administer the "Spiritual Gifts" assessment for every member to take so that every member will know their spiritual gift/s and operate in the church within their gift/s. I encourage each leader to have a daily personal devotional life. I promote education, training, seminars, and workshops that will strengthen the team's capability to fulfill the Sr. Pastor's vision for the church under God. I empower others.

2. I think that the ministry leaders must be equipped with God's Word. If they don't know God's Word how can they lead God's people?

3. I do not have specific tools that I give to ministry leaders for the purpose described.

4. Training! Training! Training! Leaders are inspired to seek Christian and godly training through the local association and congress of Christian education. If I feel that God has given me a vision for the church I seek scriptural foundation to build

upon and I use it to preach on Sunday and teach at Wednesday night's Bible study.

5. I encourage ministry leaders to obtain spiritual materials (reading) for various workshops and projects as well as request their attendance to area seminars and workshops for the advancement of the gospel on a small scale leading to larger audiences.

6. I would rely on prayer together with lots of discussion and perhaps reading books together on the issue.

7. We use a spiritual gifts inventory assessment so that each leader can understand how God has specifically gifted and wired them. We also use a Meyer's Briggs evaluation to help our leaders understand who they are and how they are both gifted and wired to function within the Body.

Additionally we have at least three leadership training workshops during the calendar year. At the beginning of the calendar year, we have a "State of the Church Address" which covers the theme and focus for the year. Then in one-on-one sessions, we attempt to guide them into critically thinking about how their individual ministry plan falls into alignment with the overall plan and strategy for the calendar year. Additionally we get them to tie their ministry budgets to the annual theme.

Question: When you need a revelation from God about a particular situation in your church or ministry what do you do?

Answers:

1. Once again, the first thing I always do is seek God's face. I am very specific and deliberate with my inquiry from the Lord. Depending on the nature of the situation (public or private) I will invoke the prayer of the leaders with me. Sometimes, the matter is revealed directly to me from the Lord. Other times I may engage only my wife, associate, or a spiritual confidant or mentor.

2. The first thing I do is seek God so that He may revel to me what He would have me to do. Second I may talk to other pastors to get some of their thoughts.

3. Personal prayer and open discussion with godly leaders both inside and outside of the congregation.

4. I go to God in prayer, but I also have a mentor and other more seasoned pastors who have been nurturing me since I became a pastor. The transition from serving as a chaplain to being a pastor is a diverse one and a challenge. There are issues that come up in the church that would never be an issue in a prison and vice versa.

5. I pray for revelation regarding the situation. I wait patiently for the revelation regarding the situation. Upon receiving the revelation I implement plans of action regarding God's will. The 3 Ps (principles) for God's ultimate plan for you and the church.

6. I fast and pray. I spend intentional time in the Word. I ask God for wisdom according to James 1:5. I also seek wise counsel from a few of my mentors.

7. Knowing those who labor among us helps us to know who can be relied on. Experience helps us to monitor the events which may arise.

Question: Has there been a point in your leadership experience when you received revelation about the future of your church or ministry? What actions on your part can you attribute to receiving that revelation?

Answers:

1. Yes I have received revelation about the future of the church many times in our 12 year history. God does seem to speak to me in visions and dreams. He gives me a big picture and perspective and He allows me to see the end in the beginning. I don't think there is any specific action that God chooses to do that with me. I believe it's just how He has gifted me spiritually.

   I would say that faithful obedience to His will and His Word does seem to be a requirement in terms of His continual revelation to me. The more faithful I am in His Word and abiding in relationship the more He seems to speak, reveal and clarify.

At times I have noticed that I can get too caught up in doing the busy work of administration and ministry. It is in those times that I find myself more assuming God's will and direction instead of being intentional about listening to His voice.

2. I have found that people are influenced greatly by the administration of the Word. Subjects on stewardship and other doctrinal materials is paramount in ushering in His doctrine — the doctrine of Christ.

3. I don't know if I can really say that I have had any specific revelation in the five years that I have been pastor. I only committed myself to two years when the church asked me to stay because the former pastor was too ill and then died suddenly. I had retired from 24 years of chaplaincy, but I guess it was not God's will for me to sit back and relax yet.

It is evident that it is God's will for the church to remain a witness in the community because He has opened doors through other people who saw our plight and just stepped in and helped. I am a certified intern mentor for New York Theological Seminary and I had envisioned a younger group coming up in the church, and out of the blue I got a phone call asking me to mentor an intern who has come and gotten the youth started and her daughter joined the church and the young people "got it going on" in a spiritual way.

4. Yes. Before leaving Texas, I laid out a revelation about the future for one of the churches to establish an affordable Christian college and seminary in the East Texas region. The actions on my part that can be attributed to receiving that revelation are prayer, study, assessment, involving ministerial leadership, partnering and collaborating with other pastoral leadership, receiving confirmation from God and church.

The pastor must always be careful to avoid the future of their church or ministry being their way instead of God's way. There must always be affirmation from the Spirit of God rather than a mere drive from the flesh or self-centered ambition. Not receiving buy-in and Spiritual/Divine guidance can lead to division, conflict, stunted growth, and eventual failure.

5. When I was serving as the interim Senior Pastor I believe I received a direct word from the Lord that the church I serve had ten years. I interpret that to mean that the Lord is giving the church a ten year window of opportunity to take godly steps towards change and re-direction of ministry focus or face continued decline and possible death. I didn't do anything to receive that word from the Lord — it just came.

6. Yes I have received some revelation from God about our church. As God gives me a revelation I call the church leaders and explain it to them. Then we have a church meeting and we tell the church.

On August 14, 2012, I had the blessed privilege to share with Dr. T. J. Harris of Carthage, TX, the concept of capturing God's vision for the future. The following day Dr. Harris provided me with his thoughts on capturing God's vision for the future.

Capturing God's Vision for the Future
Dr. T. J. Harris
Carthage, Texas, August 15, 2012

With all of the sophistications of technology that are available to us I feel that it must be understood by any leader that his vision must be compatible with and reconciled to Jesus' own vision for His ministry (i.e. I am come to seek and save that which was lost — Luke 19:10); and as expressed in the Great Commission (Matthew 28:19-20).

While each person is unique in his own personality and gifts those who would capture the vision cannot become impressed with their own uniqueness. They must always be aware that our unique gifts must be compatible with the overall Body of Christ for ultimately we are laborers together with Christ (1st Corinthians 3:9).

It must be understood by those who would capture the vision that knowing the will of God is not always readily arrived at. Therefore, the vision-seeker must be prepared to spend some time in isolated seclusion and prayerful solitude. This was David's plight when he escaped to the cave of Adullam (1st Samuel 22:3). The apostle Paul states that after his conversion he conferred not with the flesh and blood neither went he up to Jerusalem; but went into Arabia for 3 years (Galatians 1:15-18).

Finally, after conceptualizing the vision, the visionary must be prepared to deal with the fact that it might not be in his future to bring the vision to full fruition. Moses did not lead Israel into Canaan. David did not build the temple. Therefore, the visionary must look at his life's work as part of a continuum in the overall plan of God's ministry. One plants and another waters but it is God who gives the increase (1st Corinthians 3:5-8).

The responses to the questions centered on the idea of capturing God's vision for the future have some common themes. Those that stand out are:

1. Prayer (along with fasting in some cases)

2. Identifying Spiritual gifts. Knowledge of one's Spiritual gift/s may very well be the greatest indicator of how God intends to use a person now and in the future.

3. Study God's Word. It is believed that God's will is contained in His Word. Capturing His Word means capturing His will.

To these I add, knowledge of one's context, and the needs of both congregation and community. The present and future ministry that God calls one to involves meeting needs and alleviating human suffering. The great revelation from these responses is that there may not be anything super Spiritual or extraordinarily mystical that a person does to capture God's vision for the future. However, as one prays, studies God's Word, operates in their area of Spiritual giftedness, and exegete their context and culture they may find themselves being captured by God's vision rather than capturing God's vision.

SPIRITUAL GIFTS SURVEY

LifeWay Christian Resources Used By Premission

SPIRITUAL GIFTS
ROMANS 12:6-8

PROPHESYING   SERVING

TEACHING   ENCOURAGING   GIVING

LEADING   SHOWING MERCY

DIRECTIONS

This is not a test, so there are no wrong answers. The **Spiritual Gifts Survey** consists of 80 statements. Some items reflect concrete actions; other items are descriptive traits; and still others are statements of belief.

- Select the one response you feel best character-izes yourself and place that number in the blank provided. Record your answer in the blank beside each item.

- Do not spend too much time on any one item. Remember, it is not a test. Usually your immedi-ate response is best.

- Please give an answer for each item. Do not skip any items.

- Do not ask others how they are answering or how they think you should answer.

- Work at your own pace.

Your response choices are:

5 — Highly characteristic of me/definitely true for me

4 — Most of the time this would describe me/be true for me

3 — Frequently characteristic of me/true for me — about 50 percent of the time

2 — Occasionally characteristic of me/true for me — about 25 percent of the time

1 — Not at all characteristic of me/definitely untrue for me

SPIRITUAL GIFTS SURVEY

_____ 1. I have the ability to organize ideas, resources, time, and people effectively.

_____ 2. I am willing to study and prepare for the task of teaching.

_____ 3. I am able to relate the truths of God to specific situations.

_____ 4. I have a God-given ability to help others grow in their faith.

_____ 5. I possess a special ability to communicate the truth of salvation.

_____ 6. I have the ability to make critical decisions when necessary.

_____ 7. I am sensitive to the hurts of people.

_____ 8. I experience joy in meeting needs through sharing possessions.

_____ 9. I enjoy studying.

_____ 10. I have delivered God's message of warning and judgment.

_____ 11. I am able to sense the true motivation of persons and movements.

_____ 12. I have a special ability to trust God in difficult situations.

_____ 13. I have a strong desire to contribute to the establishment of new churches.

_____ 14. I take action to meet physical and practical needs rather than merely talking about or planning to help.

_____ 15. I enjoy entertaining guests in my home.

_____ 16. I can adapt my guidance to fit the maturity of those working with me.

_____ 17. I can delegate and assign meaningful work.

_____ 18. I have an ability and desire to teach.

_____ 19. I am usually able to analyze a situation correctly.

_____ 20. I have a natural tendency to encourage others.

_____ 21. I am willing to take the initiative in helping other Christians grow in their faith.

_____ 22. I have an acute awareness of the emotions of other people, such as loneliness, pain, fear, and anger.

_____ 23. I am a cheerful giver.

_____ 24. I spend time digging into facts.

_____ 25. I feel that I have a message from God to deliver to others.

_____ 26. I can recognize when a person is genuine/ honest.

_____ 27. I am a person of vision (a clear mental portrait of a preferable future given by God). I am able to communicate vision in such a way that others commit to making the vision a reality.

_____ 28. I am willing to yield to God's will rather than question and waver.

_____ 29. I would like to be more active in getting the gospel to people in other lands.

_____ 30. It makes me happy to do things for people in need.

_____ 31. I am successful in getting a group to do its work joyfully.

_____ 32. I am able to make strangers feel at ease.

_____ 33. I have the ability to plan learning approaches.

_____ 34. I can identify those who need encouragement.

_____ 35. I have trained Christians to be more obedient disciples of Christ.

_____ 36. I am willing to do whatever it takes to see others come to Christ.

_____ 37. I am attracted to people who are hurting.

_____ 38. I am a generous giver.

_____ 39. I am able to discover new truths.

_____ 40. I have spiritual insights from Scripture concerning issues and people that compel me to speak out.

_____ 41. I can sense when a person is acting in accord with God's will.

_____ 42. I can trust in God even when things look dark.

_____ 43. I can determine where God wants a group to go and help it get there.

_____ 44. I have a strong desire to take the gospel to places where it has never been heard.

_____ 45. I enjoy reaching out to new people in my church and community.

_____ 46. I am sensitive to the needs of people.

_____ 47. I have been able to make effective and efficient plans for accomplishing the goals of a group.

_____ 48. I often am consulted when fellow Christians are struggling to make difficult decisions.

_____ 49. I think about how I can comfort and encourage others in my congregation.

_____ 50. I am able to give spiritual direction to others.

_____ 51. I am able to present the gospel to lost persons in such a way that they accept the Lord and His salvation.

_____ 52. I possess an unusual capacity to understand the feelings of those in distress.

_____ 53. I have a strong sense of stewardship based on the recognition that God owns all things.

_____ 54. I have delivered to other persons messages that have come directly from God.

_____ 55. I can sense when a person is acting under God's leadership.

_____ 56. I try to be in God's will continually and be available for His use.

_____ 57. I feel that I should take the gospel to people who have different beliefs from me.

_____ 58. I have an acute awareness of the physical needs of others.

_____ 59. I am skilled in setting forth positive and precise steps of action.

_____ 60. I like to meet visitors at church and make them feel welcome.

_____ 61. I explain Scripture in such a way that others understand it.

_____ 62. I can usually see spiritual solutions to problems.

_____ 63. I welcome opportunities to help people who need comfort, consolation, encouragement, and counseling.

_____ 64. I feel at ease in sharing Christ with nonbelievers.

_____ 65. I can influence others to perform to their highest God-given potential.

_____ 66. I recognize the signs of stress and distress in others.

_____ 67. I desire to give generously and unpretentiously to worthwhile projects and ministries.

_____ 68. I can organize facts into meaningful relationships.

_____ 69. God gives me messages to deliver to His people.

_____ 70. I am able to sense whether people are being honest when they tell of their religious experiences.

_____ 71. I enjoy presenting the gospel to persons of other cultures and backgrounds.

_____ 72. I enjoy doing little things that help people.

_____ 73. I can give a clear, uncomplicated presentation.

_____ 74. I have been able to apply biblical truth to the specific needs of my church.

_____ 75. God has used me to encourage others to live Christ-like lives.

_____ 76. I have sensed the need to help other people become more effective in their ministries.

_____ 77. I like to talk about Jesus to those who do not know Him.

_____ 78. I have the ability to make strangers feel comfortable in my home.

_____ 79. I have a wide range of study resources and know how to secure information.

_____ 80. I feel assured that a situation will change for the glory of God even when the situation seems impossible.

SCORING YOUR SURVEY

Follow these directions to figure your score for each spiritual gift.

1. Place in each box your numerical response (1-5) to the item number which is indicated below the box.

2. For each gift, add the numbers in the boxes and put the total in the TOTAL box.

LEADERSHIP

—— + —— + —— + —— + —— = Total

Item 6   +   Item 16   +   Item 27   +   Item 43   +   Item 65   = Total

ADMINISTRATION

—— + —— + —— + —— + —— = Total

Item 1   +   Item 17   +   Item 31   +   Item 47   +   Item 59   = Total

TEACHING

—— + —— + —— + —— + —— = Total

Item 2   +   Item 18   +   Item 33   +   Item 61   +   Item 73   = Total

KNOWLEDGE

—— + —— + —— + —— + —— = Total

Item 9   +   Item 24   +   Item 39   +   Item 68   +   Item 79   = Total

WISDOM

<u>   </u> + <u>   </u> + <u>   </u> + <u>   </u> + <u>   </u> = <u>   </u>
Item 3   +   Item 19   +   Item 48   +   Item 62   +   Item 74   = Total

PROPHECY

<u>   </u> + <u>   </u> + <u>   </u> + <u>   </u> + <u>   </u> = <u>   </u>
Item 10   +   Item 25   +   Item 40   +   Item 54   +   Item 69   = Total

DISCERNMENT

<u>   </u> + <u>   </u> + <u>   </u> + <u>   </u> + <u>   </u> = <u>   </u>
Item 11   +   Item 26   +   Item 41   +   Item 55   +   Item 70   = Total

EXHORTATION

<u>   </u> + <u>   </u> + <u>   </u> + <u>   </u> + <u>   </u> = <u>   </u>
Item 20   +   Item 34   +   Item 49   +   Item 63   +   Item 75   = Total

SHEPHERDING

<u>   </u> + <u>   </u> + <u>   </u> + <u>   </u> + <u>   </u> = <u>   </u>
Item 4   +   Item 21   +   Item 35   +   Item 50   +   Item 76   = Total

FAITH

<u>   </u> + <u>   </u> + <u>   </u> + <u>   </u> + <u>   </u> = <u>   </u>
Item 12   +   Item 28   +   Item 42   +   Item 56   +   Item 80   = Total

EVANGELISM

<u>   </u> + <u>   </u> + <u>   </u> + <u>   </u> + <u>   </u> = <u>   </u>
Item 5   +   Item 36   +   Item 51   +   Item 64   +   Item 77   = Total

APOSTLESHIP

_____   _____   _____   _____   _____   _____

Item 13 + Item 29 + Item 44 + Item 57 + Item 71 = Total

SERVICE/HELPS

_____   _____   _____   _____   _____   _____

Item 14 + Item 30 + Item 46 + Item 58 + Item 72 = Total

MERCY

_____   _____   _____   _____   _____   _____

Item 7 + Item 22 + Item 37 + Item 52 + Item 66 = Total

GIVING

_____   _____   _____   _____   _____   _____

Item 8 + Item 23 + Item 38 + Item 53 + Item 67 = Total

HOSPITALITY

_____   _____   _____   _____   _____   _____

Item 15 + Item 32 + Item 45 + Item 60 + Item 78 = Total

GRAPHING YOUR PROFILE

	Leadership	Administration	Teaching	Knowledge	Wisdom	Prophecy	Discernment	Exhortation
25								
20								
15								
10								
5								
0								

GRAPHING YOUR PROFILE

	Shepherding	Faith	Evangelism	Apostleship	Service/Helps	Mercy	Giving	Hospitality
25								
20								
15								
10								
5								
0								

1. For each gift place a mark across the bar at the point that corresponds to your TOTAL for that gift.

2. For each gift shade the bar below the mark that you have drawn.

3. The resultant graph gives a picture of your gifts. Gifts for which the bars are tall are the ones in which you appear to be strongest. Gifts for which the bars are very short are the ones in which you appear not to be strong.

Now that you have completed the survey, thoughtfully answer the following questions.

The gifts I have begun to discover in my life are:

1. _____

2. _____

3. _____

After prayer and worship, I am beginning to sense that God wants me to use my spiritual gifts to serve Christ's body by

_____

_____

_____.

I am not sure yet how God wants me to use my gifts to serve others. But I am committed to prayer and worship, seeking wisdom and opportunities to use the gifts I have received from God.

Ask God to help you know how He has gifted you for service and how you can begin to use this gift in ministry to others.

PERSONALITY TYPES

The personality test is a free 72 question online test based on Carl Jung and Isabel Briggs Myers' typology. To take and score the personality test, go to: www.humanmetrics.com/cgi-win/JTypes2.asp

Instructions: When responding to the statements, of the two responses please choose the one you agree with most. If you are not sure how to answer, make your choice based on your most typical response or feeling in the given situation. To get a reliable result, please respond to all questions. When you have finished answering, press the "Score It!" button at the bottom of the screen.

Upon completion of the questionnaire you will obtain a 4-letter type formula according to Carl Jung's and Isabel Briggs Myers' typology, along with the strengths and preferences and the description of that personality type.

My Personality Type: _____

16 BASIC PERSONALITY TYPES:

ISTJ — THE DUTY FULFILLER

Serious and quiet, interested in security and peaceful living. Extremely thorough, responsible, and dependable. Well-developed powers of concentration. Usually interested in supporting and promoting traditions and establishments. Well-organized and hardworking, they work steadily towards identified goals. They can usually accomplish any task once they have set their mind to it.

ISTP — THE MECHANIC

Quiet and reserved, interested in how and why things work. Excellent skills with mechanical things. Risk-takers who live for the moment. Usually interested in and talented at extreme sports. Uncomplicated in their desires. Loyal to their peers and to their internal value systems, but not overly concerned with respecting laws and rules if they get in the way of getting something done. Detached and analytical, they excel at finding solutions to practical problems.

ISFJ — THE NURTURER

Quiet, kind, and conscientious. Can be depended on to follow through. Usually puts the needs of others above their own needs. Stable and practical, they value security and traditions. Well-developed sense of space and function. Rich inner world of observations about people. Extremely perceptive of other's feelings. Interested in serving others.

ISFP — THE ARTIST

Quiet, serious, sensitive and kind. Do not like conflict, and not likely to do things which may generate conflict. Loyal and faithful. Extremely well-developed senses, and aesthetic appreciation for beauty. Not interested in leading or controlling others. Flexible and open-minded. Likely to be original and creative. Enjoy the present moment.

INFJ — THE PROTECTOR

Quietly forceful, original, and sensitive. Tend to stick to things until they are done. Extremely intuitive about people, and concerned for their feelings. Well-developed value systems which they strictly adhere to. Well-respected for their perseverance in doing the right thing. Likely to be individualistic, rather than leading or following.

INFP — THE IDEALIST

Quiet, reflective, and idealistic. Interested in serving humanity. Well-developed value system, which they strive to live in accordance with. Extremely loyal. Adaptable and laid-back unless a strongly-held value is threatened. Usually talented writers. Mentally quick, and able to see possibilities. Interested in understanding and helping people.

INTJ — THE SCIENTIST

Independent, original, analytical, and determined. Have an exceptional ability to turn theories into solid plans of action. Highly value knowledge, competence, and structure. Driven to derive meaning from their visions. Long-range thinkers. Have very high standards for their performance, and the performance of others. Natural leaders, but will follow if they trust existing leaders.

INTP — THE THINKER

Logical, original, creative thinkers. Can become very excited about theories and ideas. Exceptionally capable and driven to turn theories into clear understandings. Highly value knowledge, competence and logic. Quiet and reserved, hard to get to know well. Individualistic, having no interest in leading or following others.

ESTP — THE DOER

Friendly, adaptable, action-oriented. "Doers" who are focused on immediate results. Living in the here-and-now, they're risk-takers who live fast-paced lifestyles. Impatient with long explanations. Extremely loyal to their peers, but not usually respectful of laws and rules if they get in the way of getting things done. Great people skills.

ESTJ — THE GUARDIAN

Practical, traditional, and organized. Likely to be athletic. Not interested in theory or abstraction unless they see the practical application. Have clear visions of the way things should be. Loyal and hard-working. Like to be in charge. Exceptionally capable in organizing and running activities. "Good citizens" who value security and peaceful living.

ESFP — THE PERFORMER

People-oriented and fun-loving, they make things more fun for others by their enjoyment. Living for the moment, they love new experiences. They dislike theory and impersonal analysis. Interested in serving others. Likely to be the center of attention in social situations. Well-developed common sense and practical ability.

ESFJ — THE CAREGIVER

Warm-hearted, popular, and conscientious. Tend to put the needs of others over their own needs. Feel strong sense of responsibility and duty. Value traditions and security. Interested in serving others. Need positive reinforcement to feel good about themselves. Well-developed sense of space and function.

ENFP — THE INSPIRER

Enthusiastic, idealistic, and creative. Able to do almost anything that interests them. Great people skills. Need to live life in accordance with their inner values. Excited by new ideas, but bored with details. Open-minded and flexible, with a broad range of interests and abilities.

ENFJ — THE GIVER

Popular and sensitive, with outstanding people skills. Externally focused, with real concern for how others think and feel. Usually dislike being alone. They see everything from the human angle, and dislike impersonal analysis. Very effective at managing people issues, and leading group discussions. Interested in serving others, and probably place the needs of others over their own needs.

ENTP — THE VISIONARY

Creative, resourceful, and intellectually quick. Good at a broad range of things. Enjoy debating issues, and may be into "one-upmanship". They get very excited about new ideas and projects, but may neglect the more routine aspects of life. Generally outspoken and assertive. They enjoy people and are stimulating company. Excellent ability to understand concepts and apply logic to find solutions.

ENTJ — THE EXECUTIVE

Assertive and outspoken — they are driven to lead. Excellent ability to understand difficult organizational problems and create solid solutions. Intelligent and well-informed, they usually excel at public speaking. They value knowledge and competence, and usually have little patience with inefficiency or disorganization.

ENDNOTES

1   "Call Narratives," http://alelu.blogspot.com/2010/10
    /call-narratives-in-old-testament.html (accessed
    September 9, 2012).

2   Ibid.

3   "The Prophetic Call Narrative: Commissioning into
    Service," http://www.crivoice.org/prophetcall.html
    (accessed September 9, 2012).

4   Jonathan Kirch, *Moses: A Life* (New York: Ballantine
    Publishing Group, 1998), 121.

5   "The Prophetic Call Narrative: Commissioning into
    Service," http://www.crivoice.org/prophetcall.html
    (accessed September 9, 2012).

6   Carlo Carretto, *Letters From the Desert* (Maryknoll,
    NY: Orbis, 1972), 31.

7   Brady G. Green, *Shapers of Christian Orthodoxy*
    (Downers Grove, IL: InterVarsity Press, 2010), 31.

8   Ibid., 73.

9   Ibid., 125-126.

BIBLIOGRAPHY

Hamstra, Sam Jr., "An Idealist View of Revelation," in Four Views of Revelation, edited by Marvin C. Pate. Grand Rapids, MI: Zondervan Publishing, 1997.

Hohensee, Donald. *Your Spiritual Gifts*. Wheaton, IL: Victor Books, 1992.

Hutcherson, Ken. *The Church*. Sisters, OR: Multnomah Books, 1998.

Long, Jimmy. *The Leadership Jump*. Downers Grove, IL: InterVarsity Press, 2009.

Stanley, Andy. *Next Generation Leader*. Colorado Springs, CO: Multnomah Books, 2003.

Stanley, Andy. *Visioneering: God's Blueprint for Developing and Maintaining Vision*. Colorado Springs, CO: Multnomah Books, 1999.

Stanley, Paul D. and J. Robert Clinton. *Connecting: The Mentoring Relationships You Need to Succeed in Life*. Colorado Springs, CO: NavPress, 1992.

Waal, Esther de. *Seeking God: The Way of St Benedict*. Collegeville, MN: The Liturgical Press, 2001.

Willis, Avery T. and Kay Moore. *The Disciple's Personality*. Nashville, TN: LifeWay Press, 2009.

ABOUT THE AUTHOR

D r. Gerald M. Dew holds a B.A. in Sociology — Texas Southern University, M.A in Theology — Houston Graduate School of Theology, M.Div. Eq. — Northern Seminary, and a DMin degree from Northern Seminary. He serves as the senior Pastor of the Antioch Missionary Baptist Church, Chicago IL; Adjunct Professor and Doctor of Ministry Thesis Supervisor at Northern Seminary Lombard, IL; Founder and Visionary Leader of Major Impact Ministries, Inc.

Dr. Dew is married to Marva Ceaser and is the father of two adult children, Samuel and Eboni Dew.

You may email him at: Majorimpact411@gmail.com or write to him at:

> Dr. Gerald Dew
> 20650 S. Cicero #862
> Matteson, IL 60443